BEAR HUGS

FOR

FROM

She speaks with gentle wisdom.

Proverbs 31:26 GNT

BEAR HUGS FOR MY GRANDMA

Copyright © 2003 by Zondervan
ISBN 0-310-98793-8

At Inspirio we love to hear from you—your stories, your feedback, and your product ideas. Please send your comments to us by way of e-mail at icares@zondervan.com

Requests for information should be addressed to:
Inspirio, The gift group of Zondervan
Grand Rapids, Michigan 49530
http://www.inspiriogifts.com

Project Manager: Patti Matthews
Editor: Janice Jacobson
Compiler and writer: Merry E. Marter
Contributor: Michael Vander Klipp
Design: Mark Veldheer
Photography: Synergy Photographic

Printed in China
03 04 05/HK/4 3 2 1

BEAR
HUGS
FOR MY GRANDMA

inspirio™

My Grandma
gives the
best and
biggest
hugs!

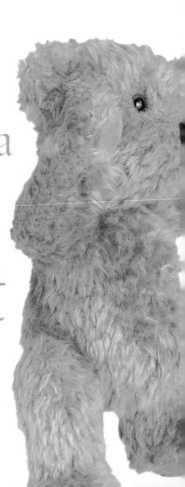

Water and sunlight are necessary for a flower to bloom. A grandma's gentle touch and unconditional love help a child grow.

GRANDMOTHER
is a word used
to describe a
magnificent woman.

No matter the
size of the task,
Grandma always
makes it fun.

The plans of the LORD
stand firm forever,
the purposes of his heart
through all generations.

Psalm 33:11

I can always count on Grandma for good advice and a fresh baked chocolate chip cookie.

The fruit of the righteous is a tree of life.

Proverbs 11:30

He has made everything
beautiful in its time.

Ecclesiastes 3:11

WISDOM

is sweet to your soul;
if you find it, there is
a future hope for you,
and your hope will
not be cut off.

Proverbs 24:14

Many women
do noble things,

but you surpass
them all.

Proverbs 31:29

Life is the flower for which love is the honey.

Victor Hugo

You will find as you look back upon your life that the moments when you have truly lived are the moments when you have done things in the spirit of love.

Henry Drummond

Few things are more
rewarding than a child's open
uncalculating devotion.

Vera Brittain

Grandmas hold
their grandchildren
in their arms and
in their hearts.

Every good and perfect gift is from above, coming down from the Father of the heavenly lights, who does not change like shifting shadows.

James 1:17

To love another
person is to see the
face of God.

Lyric from Les Miserables

No one measures up
to you, Grandma!

Love is reflected in your eyes!

What one loves
in childhood stays in
the heart forever.

Mary Jo Putney

Love is the flower of life.

D. H. Lawrence

Pleasant words
are a honeycomb,
sweet to the soul.

Proverbs 16:24

No one has ever seen
God; but if we love
one another, God lives
in us and his love is
made complete in us.

1 John 4:12

We love because
God first loved us.

1 John 4:19

May the LORD
bless you...

...and may you live to see
your children's children.

Psalm 128:5–6

"God bless you."

He did bless me, by making
you my Grandma!

I have not stopped giving thanks for you, remembering you in my prayers.

Ephesians 1:16

You are a woman of noble character.

Ruth 3:11

Sometimes
I don't have
to say
anything,
Grandma
just holds
my hand and
everything
is better.

Children's children are
a crown to the aged.

Proverbs 17:6

How priceless is your unfailing love!

Psalm 36:7

From everlasting to everlasting
the LORD's love is with those who
fear him, and his righteousness
with their children's children.

Psalm 103:17

The love we give away
is the only love we keep.

Elbert Hubbard

Your love has
given me great joy
and encouragement.

Philemon 1:7

I have loved you with an everlasting love; I have drawn you with loving–kindness.

Jeremiah 31:3

If I could put a hug in an envelope and send it to you Grandma, you would have a hug from me everyday.

Mercy, peace and love
be yours in abundance.

Jude 1:2

The fruit of the Spirit is love, joy, peace, patience, kindness, goodness, faithfulness, gentleness and self-control.

Galatians 5:22–23

Thankfu
for you
Grandm

Grandma, you are
my mentor, teacher,
role model and
best friend.
I love you!

SOURCES:

Empson, Lila, *Soul Retreats for Moms*. Grand Rapids, MI: Zondervan, 2002.

Soul Retreats for Busy People. Grand Rapids, MI: Zondervan, 2002.

Maggio, Rosalie, *The New Beacon Book of Quotations by Women*. Boston, MA: Beacon Press, 1996.

http://www.quoteland.com

http://www.aphids.com